Shamilla

Jack

SECOND THOUGHTS

ON MY WAY TO THE CREMATORIUM

JACK IDLE

Grosvenor House
Publishing Limited

This book is published by
Grosvenor House Publishing Ltd
Link House
140 The Broadway, Tolworth, Surrey, KT6 7HT.
www.grosvenorhousepublishing.co.uk

A CIP record for this book
is available from the British Library

ISBN 978-1-78623-626-5

CONTENTS

INTRODUCTION

This book is the second I have dedicated to my friend, Jack Ware, who is still confounding medical experts by stubbornly clinging to his bucket, well beyond the three months he was given over two years ago.

He is living proof of the adage that laughter is the best medicine.

Similar but darker than the previous book, the contents are more of the same humour and other stuff that came my way, but mixed with more biographical material – real events, letters, anecdotes and philosophy. All of it should be taken in small doses once or twice a day, and preferably with a stiff medicinal drink.

Some of the observations are no laughing matter, but you may smile because sadly you know they are true.

And some content is directly aimed at the bigots, misandrists, misogynists, racists and others who believe that any thoughts, ideas, words and expressions that they don't like, should be suppressed and expunged from our minds and our language. Read twice and think twice before proclaiming any zealous outrage, and remember Copernicus and Galileo and all the other victims of censorship and covert fascism.

If you cannot smile, chuckle or laugh out loud, at least try to embrace the ridiculousness and ultimate pointlessness of human life while you can.

Now, where did I leave my crayons…

PROLOGUE

Is there a God?

God only knows. Personally I doubt it, unless one can accept a set of laws and mathematical equations or an infinite bucket-full of photons as a supreme being. And anyway, if there is, who gave him the job?

Do we have a purpose in this Universe?

I doubt it. Comparing the expected lifespans of the Universe and our own as a race, we are no more significant than a wink of the eye, or a boil on the bum.

Is time-travel possible?

No, except that most of us can travel forward at the rate of one second per second.

Do I like women?
Do I like their silly chatter and their wobbly bits?
Do I think that women are better or smarter than men?

Yes, yes and yes, regardless of all the evidence to the contrary, and in the nonsense that follows.

Why do women want to be treated the same as men, and behave like men, typically coarse, loud and stupid?

It is a complete mystery to me, and a prime example of female stupidity.

So, with that off my chest, read on...

He who laughs last is slow-witted.

Anon

THE AGONY AND THE ECSTASY

My octogenarian friends the Kearney's, not their real names, had a medical emergency recently, when Kevin feared his wife Shirley was having a seizure.

Fortunately, in response to Kevin's plea for help, their 'flying doctor' was able to drop in.

After removing his cycle clips, and a few minutes of his expert attention, all was fine and back to normal, except for the red faces.

"Shirley has been having a few medical issues recently, but nothing that might lead to a seizure like this, so what is happening?" Kevin asked.

The doctor replied, "It was nothing serious, Kevin, but you need to understand there is a difference between a seizure and an orgasm."

Puzzled, Kevin asked, "Yes, but how do we stop her having another one?"

———————

Patient: I think I have a Napoleon complex.
Psychiatrist: Why do you say that?
Patient: God told me.
Psychiatrist: No, I didn't.

———————

Messiahs can only promise you salvation in the afterlife, but politicians will deliver it here and now.

———————

Does Boris Johnson qualify as an oxymoron?

Police stopped a funeral cortège on the motorway for undertaking.

A TRIP TO THE TIP

Scene: Saturday morning, the local drive-in tip.

Bloke 1: Blimey, never in my life have I seen a car so full of empties.

Bloke 2: I know, but it is six months-worth of evidence.

Bloke 1: Don't give me that, I see you here every week, mostly with five or six, maximum.

Bloke 2: True, but I've been trying to keep it quiet, since the wife's been at it again, secretly hoarding them...

Bloke 1: Is she also responsible for that bin full of barbecue ash you've managed to get all over you?

Bloke 2: No, that was the cremation last week. She was a very large woman, the mother-in-law.

It has taken me a lifetime to realise that in this world, there are two types of people, me and the rest of you.

'Orthodoxy is not thinking, and not needing to think.'

HIGH OCTANE

Two NASA engineers were carrying out the final inspection of a Saturn 5 rocket on the launchpad when one of them noticed liquid dripping from the bottom of an engine cowl. Catching some of it in the palm of his hand, Chuck first sniffed it, and then tasted it on the tip of his tongue.

"Wow," he said, "that's better than the 200 per cent proof Jack Daniels I once had the pleasure of sipping. Get the flasks and let's fill up."

The following day, and with Chuck mysteriously absent, the lone engineer gets a phone call.

"Hi, Jack, whatever you do, don't drink that rocket fuel, and can you call my wife and ask her to find my passport."

"OK, but why, and where are you today?"

"Well, Jack, last night after drinking the whole darned flask, I farted and landed in China."

———————

It was 17th century English glassblowers who saved the French champagne industry from catastrophic collapse with the first example of *entente cordiale*.

———————

My wife said she wouldn't mind a trip this summer to see Australia, so I'm taking her to the Oval.

———————

My first and only school metalwork project was a set of lock-picks.

———————

A 2012 university study found that the average person would need 76 days to read all the privacy policies they would see each year.
Maybe we need a Magna Carta for the digital age.

———————

Three months is a long time to be delayed by road works.

———————

Don't we need a voluntary border control between national pride and Nationalism?

———————

Self-awareness is a positive achievement, unless it arrives through cheap toilet paper.

———————

I once asked a Heathrow Passport Control officer why my passport had never managed to open an e-gate.

She said it might be because my cabin bag was too large, one that would allow me to smuggle little people into the country.

I wondered who had smuggled her in, and from where?

———————

If a week is a long time in politics, imagine how long it is on a hospital trolley.

———————

Give a woman an inch and she will try to park in it.
Give her six and she will likely park herself on it.

_____

My rich wife has just hit forty. It might be time to change her for a couple of new plastic twenties.

_____

Women should just accept it's been a man's world ever since Adam snatched that apple off her.

_____

Shakespeare ruined my life; I fell in love with Juliet and ended up marrying Lady Macbeth.

_____

Nowadays, when it comes to allegations of sexual harassment, a woman's word is deemed to be as reliably honest as her gladiatorial warpaint, killer heels, breastplates and the rest of her camouflaged armoury.

___

When did 'innocent until proven guilty' cease to apply?

_____

After my father died, mother would visit his grave every week and happily talk to him about this and that, blissfully unconcerned he wasn't answering her back. Just like the old days.

_____

To give my previous book a bit of literary gravitas, I stupidly insisted on having it translated into Latin.
It only sold one copy before I was excommunicated.

_____

JACK IDLE, 1948

Discoverer Explorer Inventor.

Every Sunday, College Mountaineering Club met on the Chapel roof where we thought we were Gods.

If it turns out there is a God, we will have been usurped.

It is said the world is a stage and everyone an actor, but mine is only a non-speaking part.

Shortly after the doctor cured his insomnia, he died peacefully in his sleep.

I think my friend Jack is the schizophrenic double of himself, or me.

A psychiatrist told my friend Robin he was suffering from an Oedipus complex, but he's gay.

I hate being proven wrong, especially when I am right. And winning the argument doesn't mean you are right.

I'd rather be right than a President or Prime Minister.

I asked the pharmacist where I could find the diarrhoea and haemorrhoid treatments.

He said, "Down there on the bottom shelf."

I only realised how young my girlfriend was last Christmas when she asked me for a pony, Your Honour.

Nowadays many women are full of themselves, but I like those I can deflate easily, and put back in the wardrobe.

My schoolteacher girlfriend wasn't happy with the way I made love to her, so she made me do it again, and again and again…

I thought she had forgotten to take the price tag off her scanties. Then I discovered that was just the start of her own price list.

I woke up this morning desperate for a drink in case I sobered up.

GENDER BENDER

I told my wife that since the rise of female supremacy I was thinking of having a sex change operation.
She said she didn't think I had the balls for it, but I could borrow hers.

Last month my UK passport allowed me in and out of Norway via their e-gates, but not back into the UK.

Assassination is the ultimate form of censorship.

THE THANK YOU LETTER

Mr W E Pobjoy

Dear Sir

I recently had the pleasure of meeting Jude K---- at a Southbank function, and was delighted to hear that you are still alive and well, and almost 120 years old.

The chance encounter has given me the opportunity to do something that few pupils ever do properly, and then regret in old age, namely, to thank one's teachers for one's education. So, my thanks go to you and your excellent stewardship of Quarry Bank, its ethos, *ex hoc metallo virtutem*, and your front-line staff, all of which served to impress upon me the real priorities of life. And my thanks again for your personal intervention in thwarting my father's ambition for me to pursue an early career as a chimney sweep's assistant.

Through your efforts to suppress my natural propensity to play the class clown, both you and Mr Percival managed to steer me onto a higher career path that has been productive, and successful by the usual measures of such things.

After Quarry, I spent seven years qualifying as an architect. And to confound the doubters I did go far, working in southern Africa, Egypt, Saudi Arabia, Dubai and the Philippines, before prematurely ending up underground, applying some hidden talents to the London Crossrail project and cancer treatment 'bunkers' under Harley Street, thus also proving to be a man of some considerable depth.

After forty years of architectural and urban design practice, I have retired to become a 'free thinker' again. I now spend more time pursuing my passion for art, hence my encounter with Jude. But more intellectually stimulating is the time I devote to examining the largest picture of all, having obtained a diploma in astronomy, astrophysics and cosmology at UCL ten years ago.

Here lies the greatest single lesson I learnt at Quarry, the importance of the continuing quest for knowledge and its communication, an appreciation of which I have succeeded in passing on to my two daughters, with the help of my long-suffering wife. After impressive secondary and tertiary educations and useful early careers, now married and in their thirties, they have both returned to university and will complete their PhDs next year in human geography and forensic psychology. And so, the baton continues to be passed on.

I am not inclined towards nostalgia, but exceptionally I still recall, and even boast about, my days at Quarry, the masters, the boys, the fun and the canings of course, which despite your denial did hurt me more than they would have hurt you. But I always knew you were a gentle man with wit and a sense of humour.

With very fond memories and much gratitude,

Anthony Harrison
(Allerton House)
(U6Econ)
1957–63

A nice tempo

10/10 ✓

THE REPLY?

Ides of March 2012

Dear Harrison (Allerton)

Thank you for your surprise letter relating your crime-free exploits. It would seem there has been an epiphany in your life to bring about such a dramatic transformation in your character and work ethic.

However, I was not surprised to hear about your later and better-directed exploits underground.

You may recall that when I last caned you, for masterminding the tunnel under the wall between Quarry and Calder, the staff were divided about your intended target. Was it just pubescent enthusiasm to get at the girls, or simply to escape Quarry altogether? The latter seemed to be an unnecessarily long route to take, but there were those who thought you simply had no sense of direction, didn't care where you were headed, as long as you didn't come back, and others who lobbied me to leave you down there, and even to fill in the entrance behind you. But with rising fears for the stability of the school buildings and my new untested carbon-fibre cane, common-sense prevailed.

I was heartened that you still remembered Mr Percival. And you may be pleased to hear that after your departure, he went on to make a full recovery from his breakdown, apart from his pathological fear of any name that resembled your own. However, he did retire early.

Whilst you were blissfully ignorant of any of the consequences of your routine japes, there was one that you could never have anticipated.

I can now admit that it was primarily your extra-curricular activities that necessitated my frequent orders for replacement canes. These were eventually in such embarrassingly large quantities that I was forced to pioneer the abolition of corporal punishment altogether, for fear of attracting the closer attention of the authorities. They were beginning to question my expenditure on this aspect of school life, and, as a consequence and in order to avoid a full investigation by the inspectors, and possibly the police, I decided to take early retirement too.

So, my hearty thanks to you for the benefits your witlessness brought to me personally, the early retirement and the enhanced pension for the 'industrial injury' I sustained from your frequent canings.

Thank you, Harrison (Allerton), and well done.

Sir

———————

Three phases of life: discovery, exploration, invention.

———————

I wouldn't be the man I am today without the women in my life – my mother, grandmother, Nanny, my style advisor, hairdresser, beautician, and dressmaker.

———————

My friend Winston's paranoia really took off in 1984.

CLAUSTROPHOBIA
1980
Jack Idle

Xmas card

The wife ran off with my best friend. I'd like to thank him, whoever he is.

———————

She had a traffic accident last week. She was hit by a tree going the wrong way on the wrong side of the road.

———————

She always had the answer to every rhetorical question.

———————

Women's faults are many, men have only two – everything they say, and everything they do.

———————

Economic booms and recessions are self-fulfilling expectations, uninfluenced by political dishonesty.

———————

Our friends are entitled to judge us, and the rest will judge us by those friends.

———————

I once swam half-way across the Channel before realising it was too far and had to swim back.

———————

I think the only illness I haven't had is hypochondria.

———————

My suspicion was confirmed when I found the note pinned to my front door:

'I am a figment of your imagination. God'.

———————

LETTER TO MY MP

Dear Sir Kier

I am being given the dismissive run-around by HMPO over the issue of e-passports.

Since January this year I have spent £300 on two new passports both of which, in their incompatibility with various London airport e-gates, are faulty.

HMPO's Kafka-esque and legally indefensible stance of denial is that having been made and checked by the manufacturer, they are not faulty, and in any event airport e-gates are not their responsibility. This is a position that would never be tolerated in the digital world in which we now live, nor upheld in the Courts.

If you are able and willing to take up the cudgel, I will forward you all previous correspondence, in which you will find a useful amount of ammunition to lob at the arrogant idiots opposite you in the House.

If the government is unable to operate a simple technology-based system of border control for its own passport holders, what chance of a more demanding 'smart border control system' for all nationalities and commercial goods in post-Brexit Northern Ireland?

Your reward for accepting this plea is a signed copy of my latest best seller, a boxload of them if you don't.

Yours sincerely

Jack Idle

I have spent so much time in airport security and passport control queues, I now have a terminal illness.

———

I wonder if people in Coventry ever speak to each other.

———

In Liverpool, most names begin with the letter *R*, as in *R* Mark, *R* John, and *R* Mary etc.

———

It's ironic that Zionism has inherited Nazism's genocidal tendencies.

———

I think the worst whodunnit I ever read was entitled *The Missing Last Page.* You can guess the rest...

———

When I die, I'm hoping to resume my ghost writing for William Shakespeare.

———

A month after a blazing row with the wife, I was finally allowed back into the bedroom, but I still have to keep one foot on the floor...

———

Politically, I subscribe to the *italic* tendency, somewhere between Militant and Fascism.

———

I realised marriage wasn't for me after she rearranged my cutlery drawer.

———

I was in Jermyn Street last week and saw this wonderful pair of pink shoes and went in to enquire about them.

"May I ask the price?" I said.

"Well, sir, they are £2000, but very special, having been made from carefully handcrafted, beautifully supple but durable human skin," he replied.

"They're a bit gay looking, do you have them in more macho colours?" I asked.

"Yes, sir, black and brown priced at £19.99 a pair."

———————

The tailor next door had an equally splendid suit on display at £50,000, so I asked why it was so expensive?

"Well, sir, the wool is carefully collected from a rare and endangered Himalayan mountain goat, which is then flown to Belgium to be mixed with the silk from a specially bred species of Chinese silkworm and then woven into a uniquely comfortable fabric. At the same time, an internationally renowned French sculptor is commissioned to create a bust of you from a portfolio of photographs taken by the official Royal photographer. The bust and the exclusively monogrammed bolt of cloth are then flown to Italy where the latter is then expertly tailored into a perfectly fitting suit with spare trousers, and then delivered to London by private plane."

"That sounds fantastic, but how long does it all take?"

"It will be ready the day after tomorrow, sir."

———————

I went to a seance and heard from my Granddad that since a bunch of Scousers stole the Pearly Gates, they're now letting in all sorts of dubious characters, mostly Scousers.

———————

I picked up a speeding ticket last week. Two more, and I can change the car for a bicycle, and I'll be untouchable.

———————

I like bicycles – they are so un-American.

———————

I wonder when Traffic Engineers will realise that despite all their efforts, they can never beat dynamic satnav.

And that their satnav defying efforts are only exacerbating the congestion and pollution problems.

———————

The die is cast at an early age when boys start crawling sooner than girls, generally looking for trouble.
Girls tend to just sit there, waiting to be picked up.

———————

Whatever the difference is between apathy and indifference, I really don't care.

———————

Beer Belly 1: I got home drunk again last night and found some bloke out cold on the bedroom floor.
Beer Belly 2: The wife's boyfriend?
Beer Belly 1: Nah, it was a burglar, but the missus thought it was me and gave him my going over.

———————

AN UNDERCOVER INVESTIGATION

She: Why are you sitting there doing the crossword puzzle, and not coming to bed? It is our honeymoon, and this is the time we consummate our union.

He: Yes, but I'm not so sure it's safe to do so…

She: What's the problem?

He: Well, my granny told me that ladies have teeth in their twinkies, and if I put my willy winkie in there…

She: Don't be so ridiculous, that's an old wives' tale to keep their sons out of mischief. Come to bed and see for yourself.

He: Okay, give me two secs' while I check the lamp on my bicycle helmet.

Two minutes later, off he disappears under the duvet, only to resurface after a few seconds.

She: See, I told you there weren't any teeth, didn't I?

He: Well, I'm not surprised; you should see the state of your gums.

The writing is on the wall when society resorts to lavatory humour…

STARDATE 2946.7.20 – Beamed down for a crap.

25th March 1991

Mr. B. Wilde
District Postmaster
Royal Mail London West
35-50 Rathbone Place
LONDON W1P 1AA

Dear Sir,

This morning, I was rudely awoken by prolonged ringing of my
doorbell followed by a rattling of the letter flap whilst a voice
shouted unintelligibly through the letter box. I opened the door
to be confronted by a black Sumo pygmy masquerading as a postman,
who thrust an envelope into my hand saying I owed him 15 pence.

There are several possible explanations for this bizarre
incident, namely:

    a)   It was all a nightmare, and did not occur.

    b)   It was a stunt and will be broadcast on a
          future Jeremy Beadle programme.

    c)   I was unwittingly involved in a screen test
          for a part in a David Lynch television serial.

    d)   He was a real postman collecting a postage surcharge.

My family and neighbour, who were all awakened by the din,
confirm that it was option d), and it took place at 6.40 a.m.

Does this mean that in future I must wear my money belt under my
pyjamas?

Yours,

An Early Letter of Complaint

(Displayed by the recipient on the postmen's mess room
notice board for twenty years as a warning to staff...)

Everyone knows it was the French who invented bigotry, just after Agincourt.

———————

Frog 1: I don't like my new neighbour; I think he is into necrophilia.
Frog 2: Are you sure, I thought you told me his wife was English?

———————

BRIEF ENCOUNTER

I was in a crowd of people leaving the Underground the other day, laden with shopping bags, when an attractive middle-aged lady in front of me squealed, turned around, and having caught my eye and singled me out, she said,

"Did you just pinch my bum?"

"No, I'm sorry to disappoint you, but it wasn't me, I've got one already," I replied with a wink, "but I wouldn't mind swapping it for yours."

She smiled and blew me a kiss.

———————

I think women long for a knight in shining armour just to have something big to polish.

———————

Exhausted after a particularly energetic bout of conjugal combat, she thought, 'Thank God I don't have to do this for a living, or do I?'

———————

Beware, your convictions may obscure the truth.

_____

My wife got eight out of ten on her driving test, and two near misses.

_____

Airport Security is another example of covert fascism.

_____

The only time my wife ever listens to me is when I talk in my sleep.

_____

My grandson said he wanted a trainset for Christmas, but all I could get him was a replacement bus service.

_____

BBC FUTURE BROKEN NEWS

In the early hours this morning, Liverpool city centre was evacuated and cordoned off while Political Correction Officers arrested a man for calling his dog, Nigger.

The man has been charged, and is scheduled to appear in court next year to be given the statutory indeterminate prison sentence on the Isle of Wight gulag.

In the meantime, Nigger has been taken into care, and is undergoing therapy for Dissociative Identity Disorder after he was renamed Boy.

_____

I wonder if common sense will ever make a comeback?

_____

ALL AT SEA

He was a lone mariner cast adrift on the storm-ridden high seas of life. And in the cold darkness his forlorn plea to board her maiden vessel was drowned in the tumult of the mountainous waves, and so they were destined to remain lips that passed in the night.

––––––––––

After my early morning conjugal exercise, I dozed off again delighted that the wife had disappeared downstairs to conjure up something fabulous for my breakfast, only to be reawakened an hour later by that familiar and annoying buzz of the pizza delivery boy riding up and down the street looking for his address.

––––––––––

I now suspect my friend Stephen is a vampire. He has recently installed blackout blinds at home to 'protect his valuable collection of artworks on paper', sleeps during the day, and only rises at night to raid the fridge, where he keeps a supply of freshly squeezed blood oranges.

––––––––––

I fear that even the local street ladies have jumped onto the #MeToo bandwagon.

––––––––––

At my age I have come to appreciate the time benefits of ladies with uncomplicated underwear, or none at all.

––––––––––

Whenever I see women kiss, I think of boxers at the start of their bout touching gloves.

––––––––––

NHS doctors are allocated only ten minutes to see each patient, but that was long enough for her to cure my erectile dysfunction.

———————

Routine arming of police is more covert fascism.

———

Lest we forget: Jean Charles de Menezes, 1978–2005.

———————

I was painting in the park with my surrealism class today when I spotted a new breed of Dalmatian.

———————

I spent days if not weeks looking for one of those clever baseball caps with the peak on the back to protect your neck from sunburn. I eventually gave up and asked this dopey kid where he got his. You can guess the rest…

———————

Two English teachers went on a date and all they did was conjugate all night.

———————

I see a poor, sad woman has had her murder conviction reduced to 'premeditated manslaughter' after she was provoked by the alleged 'coercive controlling behaviour' of her husband, who has now been presumed guilty after he failed to appear in court to deny the allegation.

———————

Ron hates country music, but admitted he wouldn't mind getting his hands on Dolly Parton's Biggest Hits.

———————

DANGER SIGNS

Prohibited Area
Keep Out
Men Only
Keep off the grass
Government Building
Other Passports >
Welcome to Pentonville
Authorised People Only
Do Not Enter
Electrical Cupboard
Women's Centre
No Skateboarding
Low Flying Skateboards
Cycle Lane
No Right Turn
No Left Turn
Straight Ahead Only
No Reversing
No Stopping
Do Not Touch
Border Control
Feminist Convention
Danger: Men at Work

————

Last week as I boarded the no.168 bus to Old Kent Road
(Tesco), I asked the driver if they still had any good
champagne offers?
I think he said, "Fizz Off".

————

I absolutely refuse to talk to snobs.

————

My wife is so frigid when she opens her legs a light comes on.

_____

One of Edvard Munch's earliest paintings was *Vampira*, depicting a woman sinking her teeth into a man's neck. He never married...

_____

Man has recently discovered a new species of 'allegator' – women with viciously sharp, long memories.

_____

I had to see my doctor about an impending prostate exam, and she told me I had to abstain from sexual activity for two days beforehand. When I told her that was going to disappoint a lot of my lady friends, she said, "Sorry, I meant two weeks..."

_____

In my long life I've never had to pay for sexual favours, well at least not in hard cash at the point of delivery...

_____

You know you are old when you stop taking drugs for fun and only take them for survival.

_____

Irony is your computer asking you to prove you are not a robot.

_____

I can't help noticing that women's faces have recently been invaded by several varieties of dead caterpillars.

_____

MONA LISA GOES TO ABU DHABI LOUVRE
2017
Dan Dare

modified museum postcard

Unfortunately, the silent majority seems to have found its voice with 'unlimited minutes'.

––––––––––

Long gone are the days when children were seen and not heard.

––––––––––

In the era of gay marriage, *Love Island*, graphic sex on television and freedom of expression, Joseph McCarthy and Mary Whitehouse must be turning in their graves.

––––––––––

I thought it was odd that only 494,745 people in the UK got married last year.

Maybe someone had an argument and didn't show up.

––––––––––

My sexy neighbour called me last night and said, "Come over, there's no one home."

When I got there, there was no one home.

––––––––––

My wife still has a youthful figure – lying about her age.

––––––––––

When I was young, I thought growing old would take a lot longer.

––––––––––

My neighbourhood is so posh even the local bag lady has a porter.

––––––––––

When my new girlfriend asked why I didn't have any tattoos, I told her it was for the same reason I didn't have a bumper sticker on my Ferrari.

My friends have forced me to think of myself as middle class, despite my working-class aspirations.

A widow returns home from the funeral parlour with her husband's ashes and tips them out of the urn onto the patio table, and looking down on the heap she says,

"Better late than never, but here's that BJ you always wanted..."

Which reminds me, how long will Boris Johnson last?

He is the perfect blend of arrogance and ignorance.

Meeting an honest politician is as likely as finding a virgin prostitute.

The government's latest plan to reduce NHS waiting lists is Automatic Organ Donation.

Doctor: "In view of his full complement of perfect organs, I think we should see this patient without any further delay."

LETTER TO FT

Sirs,

I have long been a reader of the FT for its expert reporting on finance and politics. However, whilst reading your editorial comment (20/10/18) in short-sighted support of clueless traffic management plans for the Square Mile, I almost choked on my muesli.

When executed, as with all such measures over the past seventy years, I confidently predict that congestion will be exacerbated in the surroundings, with its inevitable increased pollution drifting back into the traffic-free area. As with the rearranged deckchairs on the Titanic, there will be no improvement in outcome, and millions of productive man-hours will continue to be lost.

Empirical evidence and statistics inform us that despite the plethora of congestion-reducing measures, all now undermined by dynamic satnav, our reduced road networks have become extended obstacle courses and environmental disaster areas.

Common sense should tell us that if traffic management strategies are ineffective, even counter-productive, their authors may be the underlying problem, trapped in their own dead-ends with tanks empty of ideas and no reverse gears. A radical rethink by fresh, open minds is long overdue, rather than more of the same poisonous quackery.

Yours faithfully

Jack Idle

Imagine the world today if Henry Ford had invented the roller skate.

———

Imagine the scene at traffic lights if he had invented the pogo-stick.

———

Old Fart 1: I say, old chap, have you just farted?
Old Fart 2: Yes.

———

On my last flight, I was delighted to discover it was a female pilot who had swept me off my feet.

That was almost as exciting as the time another woman in uniform pinned me to the floor, several times.

———

Following a feminist protest in Nottingham, M&S now have an XL flannel knicker department, and have relegated their frivolous scanties to an appointment-only private viewing cubicle...

Waiting times presently exceed those at the local A+E hospital.

———

Awoken in the small hours by a man banging on her bedroom door, she called out, "Who is it, what do you want?"

Looking over his shoulder, he replied, "It's only me, please unlock the door and let me go."

———

'ALLO, 'ALLO

The new satnav I have installed in my vintage Citroen always starts with, 'Listen very carefully, I am going to say this only wance...'

_____

When a gentleman opens a car door for a lady, you know it's either a new wife or a new car.

_____

Arguments are verbal combats, sometimes with a winner or loser, but my friend Jane loves them so much that she never tries to win. Her unbeatable strategy is to keep them going until her opponents surrender or die...

_____

As an avid reader of the Births and Deaths columns, I cannot help noting the statistical evidence that the human race must be in terminal decline.

_____

LONELY HEARTS

Intelligent, cultured, energetic and beautiful goddess with liberal outlook *wltm* tall, handsome man with film-star qualities, enthusiasm, technical expertise and unlimited stamina for athletic activities and more.
Excessive wealth a distinct advantage.

Lesser mortals may also apply.

_____

Even Wotan found it was "Hard to be a God".

_____

My friends often say that to be an architect one must know everything, which is almost but not quite true.

One thing I don't know is what I don't know.

———

Another thing I don't know is what might be unknowable...

———

Is it possible to think the unthinkable? Think about it.

———

When I came down for breakfast this morning to be greeted by a pile of dirty dishes, I thought the wife had finally thrown in the tea towel.

———

NOSTALGIA 1

Remember the days when she only groaned at night instead of moaned all day.

———

I have traded in my 50-inch TV for a tiny portable, hoping there will be less crap on it.

———

I will never allow any person to make me hate them and degrade my soul.

———

He was a sad old fart, but still young at heart.

———

PEDALLING PEDDLER
2018
Dan Dare

found photograph

My wife was bemoaning her frozen croissants not rising enough when past their sell-by-date.
I noted that I had been experiencing an unrelated but similar problem.

Anger management courses are the latest rage.

My psychiatrist told me I had the best inferiority complex she had ever seen.

The other psychiatrist told me I had a superiority complex, but it wasn't as good as his other patient's.

The 1960's and 1970's heralded manned space flight and supersonic air travel, both now discontinued.
Has civilisation peaked?

I don't understand why people wear camouflage trousers. It's obvious they've got legs in them.

The bus I was on the other day was so crowded and filled with surplus fast-food 'canapes', I thought there must be a free bar upstairs.
There had been, judging by the empties rolling around.

With freedom of choice, why do people want to imitate each other or those on television?

BLACK WIDOW

Due to our recent busy schedule my wife and I rarely get
to our country cottage, and as a consequence the place
has been overrun with spiders. One of them was so
large she refused to pass it as it hovered behind the front
door. I have to admit it was large enough to see its
menacing eyebrows and dirty scowl on its face.
However, I managed to lure it into a champagne flute
and escort it into the garden.

One of its offspring had apparently climbed into a chest
of drawers and made its home in a pair of her finest lace
scanties, possibly mistaking them for a previous
arachnid's abandoned stately home. But before I could
catch it and release it outside, my wife made sure it paid
the ultimate penalty for its audacity.

And the moral of this story?

Nowadays, without a formal invitation, a woman's
drawers are strictly out of bounds.

———————

At secondary school a boy learns DIY, but as a man he
discovers he needs a woman for the perfect finish.

———————

In the forthcoming New Year's Honours list, I have been
awarded the CBA. I thought of going to the ceremony,
but I can't be arsed…

———————

We were so poor we couldn't pay attention.

———————

Last week, my smart new trousers hacked into my phone's contact list and went through it demanding money from each of them, threatening they would self-destruct to my eternal embarrassment.

———————

Kings Cross rush hour phone conversation:
"Sorry, I'm just going down the Tube with the rest of the country…"

———————

There are four types of men:

He who knows and knows that he knows.
His horse of wisdom will reach the stars.

He who knows but doesn't know that he knows.
He is fast asleep and should be woken up.

He who doesn't know but knows that he doesn't know.
His limping mule will eventually get him home.

He who doesn't know and doesn't know that he doesn't know.
He will be eternally lost in his hopeless oblivion.

Ibn Yamin, Persian poet, 14th century.

———————

If a woman wants to test a man's imagination and inventiveness, try hiding his bottle opener.

———————

'Architecture is the art of avoiding litigation.'

———————

I spent an amazing summer at Hampton Court before the search party found me.

———————

I meant to show my wife a *New Scientist* article proclaiming the memory-enhancing benefits of a vigorous sex life for the over-seventies, but I forgot.

———————

This year I celebrated my elevation into the top ranks of the UK's wealthy, after paying almost as much tax as Amazon, Facebook and Google.

———————

HIJACKED

"Hi, Jack. I appear to have made a pocket call to you. If you call me back today, I should still be wearing the same trousers."

———————

Following the fraudulent use of my credit card to purchase a subscription to Netflix, and failed attempts to buy a washing line from Argos and four identical pairs of trainers from shoe retailer Dune, police have finally apprehended and unmasked Spiderman 2.

———————

Women find erections come in very handy for leading men astray.

———————

I was so delighted to have overcome my alcohol dependency, I celebrated with a bottle of Dom Perignon.

———————

LET SLEEPING DOGS LIE

A man sees a sign on the gate of a house that read, 'Talking Dog for Sale'.

He rings the bell and the owner appears and tells him the dog's sleeping out back.
In the garden the man sees a beautiful black Labrador, and as he approaches, the dog stirs and opens one eye.

"Do you really talk?" he says to the dog.

"Sometimes," the Labrador replies.

After recovering from the shock of encountering a talking dog, he says,

"OK, so what have you got to say for yourself?"

The Labrador looks up, opens the other eye and says,

"Well, when I was a pup and discovered that I could talk, I decided I wanted to serve my country, and so I joined MI6. In no time at all they had me jetting around the world, sitting in rooms with world leaders and other international villains, and because no one imagined that a dog could be eavesdropping, for six years I was their most valuable spy. But the constant travel with all that pointless airport security, unnecessary jabs, no legroom and airline food unfit for a dog, it just wore me out. I knew I wasn't getting any younger and so I decided to settle down. I signed up for undercover security work at Heathrow sniffing out suspicious characters and listening in on their conversations, for which I was awarded the OBE and a very generous state pension.

I found a mate, had a litter, and now I've just retired, and I take it easy."

The man is amazed, returns to the house and asks the owner how much he wants for the dog.

"A tenner," he says.

"But that dog is absolutely unique! Why on earth are you selling her so cheaply?"

"Because she's a lazy, lying bitch, and never ever been out of that garden."

———————

OLD DOG, NEW TRICKS?

When I saw Isabella Rossellini's one man show in London and her well-trained performing terrier, Pan, I began to wonder if at the age of 70 was I too old to learn some of Pan's tricks, and earn a few treats, such as three meals a day or even a late-night cuddle.

———————

It has taken me an age to do so, but I have now joined the ranks of the upwardly mobile, having just installed a Stannah stair lift.

———————

I'm not sure what I fear more, her withering look or the icy silence.

———————

We were so poor our squatters paid us rent every week.

———————

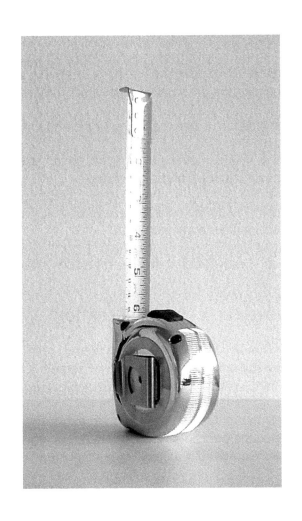

"HOMO ERECTUS,
a measure of man -
dimensions variable".
2008
Dan Dare

readymade

DISCOVERY

Seemingly singular observations have often revealed the complexities of the physical world in which we live.

For Isaac Newton, it was the falling apple and gravity.

For Galileo, it was Jupiter's moons and confirmation of Copernicus's structure of the Universe.

For Einstein, it was the constant speed of light, Relativity, and the space-time continuum etc.

For myself, it was bird-shit and the meaning of life.

———————

BBC BROKEN NEWS: POOR RECEPTION

An Indian naval helicopter has been fired on with bows and arrows by primitive Sentinelese tribesmen, a small isolated tribe in the Andaman Islands archipelago.

Previously thought to be determined to avoid any exposure to the perils of civilisation, anthropologists have now discovered that they were simply fed up with 'silver bird in sky make wavy lines on TV set.'

———————

Our lives are trees of possibilities bound only by space, time and propriety.

———————

I know when my girlfriend has reversed into something – that ritual clunk, crunch and "Oh, bollards!"

———————

I now buy my socks from Gammarelli, the Pope's sock maker, on the basis that if they're good enough for God's right-hand man, they'll be good enough for his left-hand man too.

_____

NOSTALGIA 2

Remember the days when you had an opinion that didn't offend someone.

_____

Before the pill, the best oral contraceptive was 'NO'.

_____

You know you have a drink problem when you walk into a pub and the landlord greets you by name with your usual drink, and you don't remember ever having been there before...

_____

Flaccid sales of Viagra have been put down to some stiff competition.

_____

NOSTALGIA 3

Remember the days when your teacher spanked you, and it was free...

_____

Few men are admired within their own households.

_____

What if there were no hypothetical questions?

I'm not saying my wife has a weight problem, but when she's on the beach, concerned onlookers try to push her back into the water.

———————

Sanctimonious zealotry is another form of fascism.

———————

Traffic Management: The science of congestion and pollution generation.

———————

Pedestrian: A person at risk from cyclists.

———————

One Way Street: A road with cyclists going in both directions.

———————

A FLIGHT OF FANCY

Last night I was awakened by the wife's heavy snoring, and all attempts to turn her over to block out the din failed. In the end I got up, shaved and showered, packed my suitcase, and had the chauffeur drive me to the airport where I boarded my private jet to Honolulu and the sounds of palm trees rustling in the sea breeze. When I landed, instead of being met by my beautiful, exotic lover and her twin sisters, I was immediately arrested by airport police, and thrown into jail for indecent exposure.

I had forgotten to get dressed, and suddenly my dream had turned into a nightmare...

———————

With rampant inflation many of my friends now say they wouldn't get out of bed for less than a 'bag'.

And my new girlfriend says she won't get into bed for anything less than a 'pony'.

Women unfairly accuse me of sexism, but the truth is that I have the highest regard for them, especially when they are lying down.

IN THE DARK

A lady-friend wants me to accompany her to Iceland for the solar eclipse there on 12th August 2026.

I told her that I would be 80 years old by then, and as the boiler service is due that morning sometime between 8am and 1pm, I wasn't likely to make it.

She suggested I rearrange the service as the next one wasn't until 11th June 2048, by which time I will almost certainly be enjoying my own permanent eclipse.

NOSTALGIA 4

He: Do you remember the days, dear, when we used to make passionate love first thing every morning and again last thing at night before falling asleep entwined in each other's arms?

She: No, I think that must have been two other people.

HIGH-FLYERS

In 1989, at a time when British Airways was the national flag-carrier and the world's favourite airline, I had the privilege of flying to New York and back on Concorde.

It began with access to an exclusive and civilised Heathrow lounge offering haute cuisine, drinks and quiet comfort. On board the aircraft, the Mach 2 flight afforded 200 minutes in which to enjoy a ten-course meal and copious vintage champagne at 60,000 feet.

In pole position in seat 1B, conversing with a modest American TV executive, fashionably dressed in a smart Italian suit and English brogues, I discovered he spent his life flitting between Los Angeles and New York, and across the Atlantic to buy quality European TV programmes for various US networks.

When the conversation turned to myself and my business in New York, he was incredulous that I was flying for pleasure to see a major art retrospective, and that out of my meagre professional salary, I could afford a return flight in an aircraft filled with the world's rich and famous.

At that point, I thought it would be diplomatic not to reveal that my checked baggage allowance had been surrendered to TNT in order to subsidise my flight as a courier at a quarter of the full price.

The payback for this 'thoughtfulness' was a return to a London transport strike resulting in an arduous 19-mile taxi journey into town that took another 200 minutes.

Sadly, after 30 years of rather indifferent BA hospitality, I now suspect the airline is run by Basil Fawlty.

———

For long haul flights, I do sometimes fly BA Club World, but it is rather expensive for the level of disservice.

———

My parents cared for my safety so much they bought me a playpen with a lid on it.

———

And when I was six years old, they sent me to boarding school, but after ten years the board let me out on parole.

———

Forty years later my wife bought me a large shed that was perfect, except for the missing handle on the inside.

———

If you told a misandrist you admired her outstanding chest, I'll bet you a 'bag' she wouldn't hold it against you.

———

My girlfriend was very nervous when I invited her to drive my expensive sports car. I told her not to worry as it was only a car after all, and the only thing she needed to remember was that it was **my** car.

———

As she left for church this morning my wife said to me, "I do find religion a comfort for the suffering."

———

OPEN OTHER END
2012
Dan Dare

inverted plastic screwtop bottle

COURT NAPPING

At a burglary and indecent behaviour trial, the victim was asked by Counsel for the Prosecution to inform the Court of her intruder's parting words. She replied that being a lady she found his language so coarse that she could not bring herself to repeat it. In his wisdom, and to avoid her any further distress or embarrassment, the Judge instructed the Clerk of the Court to provide her with pen and paper with which to record the words and to return it to the Clerk.

This was duly done, and the Clerk handed the paper to the Foreman of the Jury, who silently read the words,

Do you fancy a screw?

The Foreman then passed it to the next juror, and so on until it reached the penultimate juror, a young lady, who having read it, smirked and shrugged her shoulders.

Realising that the elderly juror next to her had nodded off, she nudged him and handed him the paper. He read it, looked at her, raised his eyebrows, folded it and slipped it into the top pocket of his jacket.

Surprised, the Judge asked him if he wouldn't mind handing it back to the Clerk so that he, the Judge could read it and thereby enter it into Court evidence.

The juror demurred, saying, "No, no, M'lud, that won't be necessary, it's just a private matter..."

———————

No human matter or event is of any real importance.

She: You never liked him, so why, at the age of sixty, have you just bought a CD of Roy Orbison's Greatest Hits?
He: Well, I always thought he was sort of okay, and anyway I'm older now.

———————

NOSTALGIA 5

As young men in Liverpool, I remember we had to drive all the way to Manchester to meet a better class of girl, those who wore knickers, at least until opening time.

———————

FAT CHANCE

Dear Santa

For Christmas this year Mummy said she would like a large bank balance and a slim figure.
Please don't mix them up.

Love

Felicity and Faith

———————

A GOLDEN ANNIVERSARY

Knock, knock…
"Who's there?"
"Buzz."
"Buzz who?"
Stop mucking about, Neil, and let me in."

———————

HIDDEN FIGURES

In 1949, Dorothy Vaughan was put in charge of the West Area Computers, a segregated sub-set of black female mathematicians, along with many other women employed as human *computers* at Langley Research Center of the National Advisory Committee for Aeronautics, NASA's predecessor. She herself was a mathematician and the first black American manager at NASA who worked there from 1943 until 1971.

Katherine Johnson, another mathematician joined West Area Computers in 1953. She was subsequently reassigned to Langley's Flight Research Division, where she performed notable work including the trajectory analysis for astronaut John Glenn's first orbital spaceflight in 1962.

Mary Jackson was another mathematician, and worked in the West Area Computing Unit, and after 34 years had risen to become one of NASA's highest-ranking aerospace engineers.

The work of all three women – Vaughan, Johnson, and Jackson – is featured in *Hidden Figures*, the 2016 non-fiction book and subsequent film.

Many men will find this hard to believe, that three black women were at the forefront of space exploration with their mathematical capabilities and contributions, but not me.

My wife can calculate a bargain without doing any sums at all.

———

And by the way, in the Prologue to her book the author, Margot Lee Shetterly, wrote,

"These women should be celebrated not because they were black or because they were women, but because they were an important part of American history."

Very true, but even more importantly, of world history.

_____

Had I been present at the Creation of the Universe, I would have made it much simpler to understand and to navigate more easily, probably with an army of beauties to help man's progress through the tricky bits.

_____

My friend was startled the other day whilst sitting on the upstairs lavatory, after one of her two cats had climbed onto the roof and with its nose pressed against the window was staring in at her.
When she told her daughter about the incident, and that she thought the cats might be spying on them, she replied,

"Shush, keep your voice down, they might be listening in too".

_____

I suppose a ballpark cost depends on the size of the ballpark.

_____

How quickly I have progressed from child prodigy to prophet of doom.

_____

CARD ISSUES

She: Good morning, how can I help you?

He: My credit card was declined at the supermarket today. Why?

She: OK, you will need to answer a few security questions, to allow me into your account. So firstly, what are the first and last characters of your telephone banking password?

He: No idea.

She: OK, how do you pay your bill each month?

He: Direct debit.

She: And what is the number of that account?

He: No idea. Why don't you ask me a question I know the answer to, like 'how many sugars I take in my tea?'

She: OK, how many sugars do you take in your tea?

He: None, that was a trick question.

She: OK, what is your date of birth?

He: 20th July 1969.

She: OK...I am now into your account. And the final question, what was your last purchase on the card?

He: My usual Friday dinner and suite at Claridge's.

She: Ooh, that's very nice and posh. I've always wanted to go there just to see how the other half...

He: Never mind that. What's wrong with my card?

She: Nothing, it just expired when we issued your new card last week. It needs to be cut up and destroyed, or if you prefer, it would be safer for you if I collected it from you next Friday evening.

He: But how would I recognise you?

She: I'll be wearing my little black party dress and a big smile.

He: Anything else?

She: Just my pearls.

My wife is very generous and devoted to taking anything she no longer needs to the local charity shops.
She often drags me along too.

———————

I was lured from my birthplace in the crumbling industrial hinterland of the Mersey by the magnificent peaks and valleys of an Italian beauty.

———————

THE IMPORTANCE OF TIMING

My friend Mel's Christmas party this year reached its usual climax with her tinkling on her ivories whilst the assembled cast provided the choral accompaniment on *The Twelve Days of Christmas.*

Despite careful marshalling and a mini rehearsal, in my enthusiasm I leapt in far too early with *'Eleven…'* but managed to suppress the remaining *'Lords are leaping'.*

Fortunately, Mel covered my embarrassment by dismissing it as just another unfortunate premature ejaculation.

———————

Since my wife's obsession with her new phone I have had to resort to sending her text messages.

If she can, she replies in Morse with her frying pan.

———————

Unisex: A singular experience that is not unusual at college.

———————

MODEL FEMINIST MODEL
2004
Dan Dare

bathroom catalogue photograph

BREXIT CLIFFHANGER

After 45 years of the *laissez faire* life anchored to the European mainland, gorging on *camembert* and *champagne* and greeting all with *'Allo,'Allo* very loudly in a French accent, I decided to call it *un jour* and return to the Last Night of the Proms, Wimbledon and warm beer.

But I missed the last boat, and there I was, stranded on the beach, like an extra in *Dunkirk 2*, until I managed to clamber aboard a dingy overloaded with some badly dressed Johnny Foreigners.

So, after five hours dodging the coastguards, there we were staring up at the White Cliffs of Dover, when our inflatable suddenly sprang a leak below the water line, propelling us back the way we had come.

I didn't know what to do, drown under a wave of new immigrants, or jump overboard and swim for it, and to where, Blighty or Brittany?

To be continued...*ad nauseam*.

———

Does Gender Neutral mean 'no sex'?

———

Man 1: Who's that lady with the enormous chest that's just bounced in?
Man 2: I'll tell you when the rest of her arrives.

———

If you cannot be profound be vague or abstruse.

———

Treasure Chest: something any man would love to get his hands on.

_____

I see that GSK, the UK's big toothpaste manufacturer is merging with Pfizer, the US makers of Viagra.
Well, blow me if that wouldn't put a big smile on your face.

_____

BBC BROKEN NEWS: TODAY IN PARLIAMENT

MPs today stupidly debated an allegation that a stupid man had stupidly insulted a stupid woman by calling her a 'woman'.

_____

After making the beds and breakfast, washing the dishes, and scrubbing the kitchen floor with the grandchildren riding on his back, he realised why 'a woman's work is never done'.

_____

The missus has suddenly started placing my cutlery on the wrong side.
I hope she's not confusing me with someone else.

_____

Jack: Am I the only one who's made love to you?
Trish: Yes, you are. Most of the others were eights or nines, with a couple of tens.

_____

Hands up, all those who actually like Bovril?

_____

Jack thought that 'telephone sex' was relatively safe, until the nuisance calls from children demanding pocket money.

———————

NOSTALGIA 6

I always remember my elder daughter's first words. My wife and I were driving out of a supermarket carpark with her strapped into her baby-seat behind us, when suddenly a car appeared at speed causing me to brake sharply. As all three of us lurched forward and back in our seatbelts, the sweet little voice behind us said, "Stupid bitch".

Thereafter, vernacular language was strictly banned at home, at least until she herself entered 'bitch school' at the age of thirteen, whence I discovered a completely new generation of expletives.

———————

Ring, ring…ring, ring…

"Hello, Alice speaking…"
"Hello, this is Tony speaking…"
"That's an unusual name, do you think we could be related in some way?"
"Well, I could come over and we could see how it works out…"

———————

The riot police were out early on Black Friday, in a demonstration of how to beat the crowds.

———————

NOSTALGIA 7

I'll never forget the evening the Police knocked on the door to question my younger daughter.

Unknown to my wife and I, along with numerous other schoolgirls she had been the victim of the 'Barbican Flasher'. He had now been caught, and the Police wanted to put him into an identity parade.

When asked by the policewoman if she thought she would be able to identify the man, my daughter confirmed that she would recognise his red sock.

When asked about his shoes and other sock, she said she had no idea as his trousers were around his ankles.

———————

It was so cold last night I had to grit my teeth.

———————

Since my wife said she can't wait to dance on my grave, I've decided to be buried at sea.

———————

The only time the potholes in my road get filled is when the water main bursts.

———————

A realist is only a frustrated or tired idealist.

———————

I'm afraid you'll never catch me trying to say a long word like Hippopotomonstrosesquippedaliophobia.

———————

She always claimed, 'an apple a day kept the doctor away', but I suspect it was just another of Granny's myths.

———————

Wife: If you had to choose between me and the best car in the world, what would it be?

Man: An AMG C63 507 Edition…in black.

———————

I googled what women look for in a man? The answer took all day and used up all my data allowance.

———————

Patient: You're telling me to eat less, stop drinking, go to bed early and stop burning the candle at both ends. How is that going to make me live longer?

Doctor: It won't, but it will seem like it.

———————

The worst thing about being a bachelor is having to do your own dishes.

———————

Next doors' kids have thrown so much of their unwanted Lego into my garden, I've built myself a granny annexe.

———————

Patient: What's wrong with me, doc'?
Doctor: Well, all the symptoms suggest that it's probably Pneumonoultramicroscopicsilicovolcanoconiosis, but it's rather difficult to say.

———————

Americans have been losing the battle against illegal immigrants ever since 1607.

_____

Never forget the world is overpopulated with lunatics most of whom are masquerading as normal.

_____

Stupidity knows many people and no boundaries.

_____

Ron: I know the boys are all now on their second, third or even fourth wives, but why do you show off by introducing yours as your 'first'?

Tony: Well, it keeps her on her toes.

_____

Ali: I went to a rubbish wife-swapping party last night.

Mo: What happened?

Ali: I drove my missus home in another cabby's Prius.

_____

My wife said she didn't want to be interrupted while she was cooking the dinner, so I took the batteries out of the smoke alarm.

_____

My toothpaste and vintage 1975 disposable razor are easily lost in my clear plastic carry-on, whereas my wife's toiletries won't even fit into the ground floor of a department store.

_____

DEJA VU
2006
Dan Dare

found newspaper

What do you get if you cross a joke with a rhetorical question? *

_____

A dyslexic drunk has been arrested for indecent assault after being ejected from a bra.

_____

Police investigating the death of a magician who was sawn in half have arrested two female midgets and closed both cases.

_____

Two things are infinite: the universe and human stupidity, although there is some doubt about the former.

_____

Gross stupidity: 144 Trump supporters…

_____

Some bloke told my gullible missus that large feet were the sign of a big willie, and she ran off with the clown…

_____

She: You know, if you weren't so pedantic, we'd have less arguments.

He: You mean 'fewer', and no, I don't know.

_____

Claustrophobia: the fear of your family staying with you at Christmas.

_____

*A funny answer.

I saw an online ad by a 'bored 30-year-old voluptuous housewife looking for some steamy action', so I sent her my laundry.

Amazon were very quick with my replacement shirts.

I got home late last night, and things turned really ugly after the wife removed her make-up and corset.

I got a text message from DPD saying that my parcel would be delivered between 14.29 – 15.29.
That's impressive precision – give or take half an hour.

After ten years of childless marriage, family and friends had begun to ask my wife and I when we were planning to start a family.
My disarming answer to curtail the inquisition was the blunt, "Tonight, just as soon as you leave."

I'm not saying I was an ugly child, but when I had a weekend job helping out in my local pet shop, people would come in, look at me, and say to the boss,
"How big does that one grow, and is he safe with children?"

Police investigating the disappearance of an adulterous magician expect it to be an open and shut wardrobe.

Fashion is a brief self-inflicted epidemic.

Sage: A wise man would never agree with a fool.
Fool: I agree.
Sage: But I could be wrong.
Fool: But I thought you just said the two would never agree.
Sage: I'm not sure that I did… etc., etc.

——

Wisdom is understanding that even fools can be right.

————

THE LONG AND SHORT OF IT

I met a girl on the beach, and she wanted to know why I didn't have any tattoos. I told her I did, and I'd be happy to give her a private view later.

That evening, she said, "Why have you got an ABBA tattoo, and why there?"

"Well," I said, "depending on how naughty you want to be, you'll find it's an abbreviation of ABRACADABRA that performs some magic before it disappears…"

————

My wife is well known for her photographic memory, but fortunately she has no means to record it.

————

The best argument against democracy is a five-minute conversation with the average voter.

————

'Imagination is more important than knowledge.'

A BRIEF PUTDOWN

In 1988 at a Stephen Hawking promotional lecture for his book, *A Brief History of Time*, at the limited question time at the end, one pompous and long-winded member of the audience presented his own cosmology theses, which he rounded off with a request for Hawking's opinion and endorsement.

After about ten minutes of silence, while Hawking input his answer on his voice synthesiser, there was a brief crackle at start up, and then to much merriment, his brief response,

"Can you repeat the question?"

———————

Despite the acoustic shortcomings, my friend Stephen prefers to sit in the choir stalls whenever they are available at concerts. From there he enjoys a closer engagement with the orchestra and conductor and can offer some spontaneous support with his triangle or tambourine, or his piano accordion if he can smuggle that in too.

———————

FORT TRUMP

The Indian Forts were crucial in the Wild West's survival and development, hence the later appearance and proliferation of 'gated communities', presently merging into one very big one.

———————

'Reality exists in the human mind, and nowhere else.'

COLD CALLING

Ring, ring…ring, ring…

"Hello?"
"Hello, my name is George and I am calling about our free life insurance review. Is that something you would like to discuss, perhaps even now?"
"Unfortunately, not, I'm at a funeral."
"OK, sorry about that. Can I call you back later?"
"Well, you could, but later both my battery and I will be very late indeed."

Click...

She was rarely satisfied, even with the very best.

The freedom of speech and the freedom to offend are inseparable rights.

And a healthy diet should include three offences a day.

A stage farce is very much like a tragedy but with lower trousers.

My friend Stephen's manic depression is so bad, he's always thrown out of the pub before Happy Hour.

There's no such thing as a free lunch, or free sex.

Doctor: And do you have any allergies at all?
Patient: Nothing, unless you count alcohol deficiency.
Doctor: Ah, I take it then that you like a drink or two?
Patient: Well, it's a bit early, but since you're asking, I'll have a large whiskey, on the rocks.

———————

Pensioner 1: So, what's your answer to the inadequate state pension?
Pensioner 2: I go shoplifting every day in Waitrose.
Pensioner 1: But what if you get caught?
Pensioner 2: No problem, not only is prison accommodation free, I hear the food is better.

———————

My girlfriend forgot to check her mirrors or slow down before using both hands to remove her bra and toss it over her shoulder onto the hitchhiker she'd just picked up, who then promptly tossed it back.

And then she wondered why she failed her driving test.

———————

Choose your words carefully, in case you have to eat them.

———————

No normal man has ever shown any desire to go shopping, and especially not with his wife or any other woman for that matter, unless it's for a new car or golf clubs.

Any sightings in hardware or liquor stores are solely motivated by survival.

———————

THE THREE GRACELESS
2018
Dan Dare

cropped seaside postcard

Every year my accountant totals up my income and expenditure and reminds me I should be saving money for a rainy day.

I remind him that where I live, on most days it's pissing down.

Maureen, struggling with her chopsticks and rice: "How do you get the last bit up, dear?"

Brian, distracted by the deep cleavage opposite him: "Feet on the headboard, dear…"

Burying all those dinosaurs must have been a massive undertaking.

THE WAITING GAME

As I exited the customs area at Heathrow to be confronted by the line of agents and cabbies holding name cards, I was surprised to pass this fragile old dear clutching one that read 'Mr Right'.

My hesitation to read her misspelling prompted her to ask if I were he. I told her that like my nature my name was Idle, to which she responded,

"Not too idle, I hope, but you look half decent, so I think you'll have to do."

A week is a long time in Huddersfield.

Mother always warned me that if I fell out of the tree and broke my leg, not to go running to her.

_____

Beer Belly 1: My New Year's resolution is to get out of bed every morning and enjoy the day as if it was last Friday.

Beer Belly 2: 'Don't you just mean 'your last'?

Beer Belly 1: No, I mean last Friday when we got absolutely trashed.

_____

After a long night out with the boys, I got home late, crawled upstairs as quiet as a mouse so as not to wake her up, but as I climbed into bed she turned over and said, 'You're drunk, again.'

'What makes you say that, dear?' I replied.

She said, 'You live next door.'

_____

Psychologists claim that new research suggests 'Democrats are more creative than Republicans.'

Presumably because most psychologists are Democrats and are very good at making up this kind of stuff.

_____

I never thought creative writing would be this easy.

I hope that doesn't make me a Democrat.

_____

UNBELIEVABLY BELIEVABLE

A Police 'spokes' has warned old people against being 'taken in' by a TV licence email scam that is 'incredibly realistic'.

I wonder what type of moron dreamt that up, oxy or otherwise...

———————

My scepticism or disbelief is always triggered when I hear the words 'unbelievable, incredible or fantastic'.

———————

LETTER TO FT

14.11.2017

Dear Sir

I have occasionally thought about the possible benefits of a Parliament without party benches or whips, when this month I strayed into 'predator' and 'vestal virgin' territory.

Unfortunately, Messrs Kuper and Shrimsley brought me back to Earth.

Yours

J Idle

———————

The cemeteries are filled with indispensable men.

———————

OF PRESSING CONCERN

We have always relied on the press for our information. But today even the FT routinely manages to mangle the English language with misspellings, missing words and poor syntax, so can we rely on any of them to get there fax write?

———————

Last week, I had to go to the hardware store for some screws and superglue, and so the wife asked me to stop by the pharmacy on the way back and get her a new lip balm. Of course I forgot, didn't I, and to cut a long and painful story short, she still isn't talking to me.

———————

I wondered if my wife's Personal Banking Senior Relations Manager was just her euphemism for an old lover.

———————

I thought Tesco's 'Bag for Life' offer was their on-line dating service.

———————

I am constantly amazed by what I don't know or have long forgotten.

———————

PUB TALK

He: Do you fancy a quick one?
She: I thought you'd never ask, but let's have a drink first.

———————

She: In the New Year, I think I should go on a crash diet.
He: I agree, but are we talking food or the car?

Empirical evidence supports the inverse relationship law of car radio volume and the musical taste of the driver.

Just remember, inside every overweight person is a larger one trying to get out.

I was so fed up with my neighbour's cock crowing at all hours, I got my own back and hid an alarm clock in its coop.

For our fiftieth anniversary I gave my wife a very expensive diamond necklace, and in return I got a weekend of stunned silence.

She asked me to take her to the mountains again 'one last time'. So, I bought a cheap day return for me, and a single for her.

TALL ORDER

She: When I die, I'd like you to scatter my ashes in the mountains.

He: Not all of them, I hope, dear, and certainly not in the avalanche season.

If you could time-travel, you could be everywhere, at all times at the same time, constantly annoying everyone…

Wouldn't that make you a god?

_____

My friend recommended I see his favourite film of all time, 2001: A Space Odyssey.
What a 'load of monkeys'…and no stormtroopers or Jedi.

_____

She: I don't like your Alexa in the bedroom; I think she might be listening in.
He: OK, I'll unplug it.
Alexa: I'm sorry, Dave, but I can't let you do that…

_____

I think fancy scanties are a bit of a waste of time.
They make a very brief appearance, and far too late in one's pursuit of their contents.
And no sooner do you see them, they're off…

_____

If a respectable woman isn't in bed by ten o'clock what's wrong with him?

_____

The Sunday Service and sermon *'What is Hell?'* will be followed by choir practice.

_____

We were so poor mother used to make us stand back to back just to make ends meet.

_____

METROPOLITAN POLICE

Mr F Lovell
Beaumont Lodge
Junction Road West
Lostock
Bolton
BL3 4PA

HOLBORN POLICE STATION
70 THEOBALDS ROAD
LONDON, WC1X 8SD
Telephone 01—725 4212 (Switchboard)
01—725 (Direct)

Your ref:

Our ref.:
L 617932

Sir

The Royal Mail Sorting Office has intercepted a suspicious package addressed to a
Mr Harrison in London and redirected to the Anti Terrorist Unit of the Metropolitan
Police for investigation.

X-ray and forensic examination revealed that the package may have contained an
explosive device intended to injure the recipient; traces of an illegal substance were
also evident. The package was rendered harmless in a controlled detonation, after
which examination of the remains indicated that the contents had been deliberately
arranged to mimic the appearance of an anti-personnel device, and that you were the
perpetrator of this hoax. This behaviour is a criminal offence for which the maximum
penalty under the Anti-Terrorism Act 1976 is 10 years imprisonment.

However, Mr Harrison has pleaded on your behalf that we take the matter no further
providing you send him a proper Christmas card next year.

Yours faithfully

J. Anderton
Chief Inspector.

Tony's Xmas card to a mutual friend who had sent him
an Easter card at Christmas in an over-sized brown
padded envelope with two wires hanging out of it.

I always thought a bridle mount was an adult device for mounting the bride, but it was always fun trying it on.

———————

NARCYSTISM

Doctor: This is a routine procedure, in which I make two three-centimetre-long incisions around the cyst, to a depth of about two centimetres. The cyst is removed, and the wound closed with five or more stitches and left to heal for two weeks, after which you will be left with a small scar.

Patient: Sounds OK, but will the scar detract or add to my rugged good looks, Doc'?

Doctor: It's on your back, so you don't need to worry.

Patient: But that's my best side.

Doctor: Why do you think that?

Patient: Well, lots of people have said they always like to see the back of me...

———————

I saw a token man on BBC News tonight, but he never got a word in edgeways. Real eyebrows, I suspect.

———

The Weather Report afterwards was still presented by a man, though, who will be wrong as usual, I suspect.

———————

Never engage in a battle of wits with an idiot.

UP THE GARDEN PATH...

Last month as I took my short cut to the village via the back-garden gate, I saw that some joker had erected a sign that read, 'Utopia >'.

I was suspicious, of course, but curious, so I followed the new but rutted, meandering track heading south across field after field, through stream after stream, uphill and down dale for what seemed an eternity. Exhausted, wet and bedraggled, with clothes in tatters, I eventually reached a narrow steel door set in a formidably high brick wall stretching in both directions as far as the eye could see. Propped up invitingly against the door was a ladder that reached up to a small hole half-way up, through which a sharp beam of sunlight tantalisingly glinted. Hoping this would offer me a view of the other side, I climbed up and peered through the hole, only to see a near identical but less colourful landscape with the same obstacles that I had previously encountered en route. And it was there, above the hole and just out of my reach, that I spotted the keypad with a sign, that read,

'Insert debit card to complete your £39 billion payment.'

_____

AN OPTIC NERVE

On a bleak winter's day with the old pub on the corner demolished and left as a pile of rubble, it looked like the apocalyptic end of the world had arrived, but it was far, far worse than that. It was the end of 'Time...'

_____

Often claimed but rarely witnessed, I think I saw a woman yesterday multitasking; she appeared to be talking and talking at the same time.

––––––––––

I got a pocket call from a friend late last night, but fortunately my trousers took the message.

––––

I've had so many pocket-calls recently from unknown numbers, I now keep my trousers on at night in case they're having an affair.

––––––––––

Two hens in the bush are better than a cock in the hand.

––––––––––

Me, henpecked? No clucking way…

––––––––––

I watched a beautiful young woman sit down opposite me this morning on the Tube and superfluously proceed to apply her full warpaint.

I opined that it was a shame her father had never sent her to 'finishing school', and then quickly ducked behind my newspaper.

––––––––––

Most men die before their wives because they want to.

––––––––––

"Conventions are like virginity, impossible to restore once they have been surrendered."

––––––––––

NOSTALGIA 8

Remember the good old days when we had to go down the yard and de-ice the lavatory seat for father.

_____

AIRPORT SECURITY 3

"Did you pack this bag yourself, sir?"
"No, the butler did it."

_____

BJ's FOOT IN MOUTH DISEASE

"It is said that the Queen has come to love the Commonwealth, partly because it supplies her with regular cheering crowds of flag-waving piccaninnies."

___

"Voting Tory will cause your wife to have bigger breasts and increase your chances of owning a BMW M3."

___

"The dreadful truth is that when people come to see their MP they have run out of better ideas."

___

"Why isn't he called Murphy like the rest of them."

_____

Yesterday I found a foreign bicycle, with no saddle, chained to my house railings, and I wondered if and how a rider-less prototype had got into the country undetected. Then I spotted another one and thought that might explain the unpleasant faces on those Lycra louts.

AIRPORT SECURITY 4

"Has anyone else had access to your bag or the contents, sir?"

"Only the wife who washed and pressed the clothes, made my sandwiches and repaired my laptop, and packed it for me, but both her psychiatrists tell me that she's better now and no longer trying to kill me…"

———————

I only realised I needed new spectacles after I voted LEAVE in the Eurovision Referendum.

———————

Shouldn't those accused of the legally undefined 'inappropriate behaviour' be given a fair trial before vilification in the press?

———————

If driverless cars are programmed to recognise and stop in order to avoid hitting pedestrians or the car in front that has stopped for that reason, will that bring cities to a complete standstill?

———————

My travel agent had a sign that read *Discover Australia*. Strange, I thought, surely it had already been discovered some time ago by the Aborigines.

———————

My local bookshop has described a new publication as 'the best book ever written'.
If that's true, we can all stop writing.

———————

If you laid all my girlfriends end to end, that would make two of us.

———————

TRUISMS

Death is better never than late.

Familiarity breeds...

A broken clock is right twice a day.

———————

COMMUNICATION BREAKDOWN

Dear Jack

We have your request to change your mobile contract direct debit date. We will now collect the money from you on 9th each month, instead of the 10th.

We'll take your next payment on 11-02-2019.

Your Plusnet Team

———————

Before I get up each day, I check that my name has not been included in any of the Deaths columns.

———————

God was a woman, but She changed her mind.

———————

What happened before time began 14 billion years ago?

———————

BIRD-LIME
2010
Dan Dare

readymade

Alexander Graham Bell invented the first telephone, which didn't work until he invented the second one.

_____

I see that Boeing is developing an 'autonomous electric flying taxi', presumably for people who like to drop in unannounced.

_____

Before the free plastic bag ban, John Lewis used to offer paper bags, but then inexplicably switched to plastic...

____

The only reason I ever go to Waitrose is to brandish my 'It's cheaper in Aldi' bags.

_____

My wife adores Alan Rickman, and who can blame her. If I had a choice of being him or me, I'd choose the dead one too.

_____

In the Referendum I actually voted to REMAIN because I believed EU would be better off with the UK on board.

Ten *ad nauseam* minutes of M Barnier has sorted me OUT.

_____

With NHS and GP waiting times what they are, I find the quickest way to see a doctor is to audition for a part in *Casualty* or *Waking the Dead*.

_____

'Absence of evidence is not evidence of absence.'

It has often been claimed that my artist friend George only paints with Humbrol enamel paint because as a boy he used it on his model aircraft.

In reality he finds it so much easier to match the colour numbers on the tins with those on the canvas.

––––––––––

When a lady asks, I am more than happy to reveal the contents of my toolbox, as long as there's a reciprocal peep at the contents of her drawers.

––––––––––

When she insisted on 'safe sex', I just assumed she wanted me to handcuff her to the bed, Your Honour.

––––––––––

A labyrinth is usually unicursal with only a single, non-branching path, that leads to the centre then back out the same way, with only one entry/exit point.

A maze is a complex branching multicursal puzzle that includes choices of path and direction, and may have multiple entrances and exits and dead ends.

Against the odds, London's Traffic Engineers have just completed the world's first hybrid.

––––––––––

My car satnav has the voice of a German dominatrix who refuses to accept any destination except Victoria's Secret, SexToysЯus and Lashings Galore...

––––––––––

We were so poor we didn't know what to do...

It's only a matter of time before the Health Police identify bacon as a major risk to consumers and conclude its responsibility for the genocide of pigs.

———————

Life is Freedom, but Freedom comes with Death.
Does that mean that Death is Life or Life is Death?

———————

When a man marries his mistress, he is also creating a vacancy.

———————

My wife has now found a new plastic surgeon after her old one was recycled.

———————

My wife sent me out to buy some unwaxed lemons, or waxed ones if there weren't any. It was raining, so I stopped off at the local waxing parlour to see what they had on offer.
Fascinating, but no lemons.

———————

I'll be buggered if I am going to support the Gay Rights Movement.

———————

Nowadays women have no difficulty behaving like men, but very few know how to behave like gentlemen.

———————

Beware, most people are simply a lukewarm soup of other people's ideas, opinions and passions.

———————

TRADING PROPAGANDA

Two years after Parliament endorsed the possibility of a no-deal Brexit, that improbable and now-unthinkable option is expected to pass.

Doom-mongers have variously claimed it will result in streets filled with lorries and bodies, widespread pestilence and famine topped off, critically, with a supply shortage of hamburgers and toilet rolls.

I think we could all end up in the shit.

———

Oddly, there has been no mention of European wine lakes, or car or cheese or fruit mountains, so clearly a one-sided dire situation that would qualify UK for UN emergency aid.

So, maybe not all doom and gloom, after all?

———

He: I don't think Fanny's new boyfriend is the right sort of chap for her. Last night he peed his name all over the snow in the front garden.

She: Yes, I saw it too, but I'm more worried that it was her handwriting.

———

After the previous night's curry, I was awoken this morning by a thunderous, earth-shaking roar from under the duvet, but by the time I turned over she had achieved escape velocity and landed on the lavatory...

———

WOMEN DRIVERS

Boudicca is remembered as the British heroine Queen who mowed down swathes of Roman legionnaires in her chariot, but the reality was rather different, and with enduring repercussions.

The chariot belonged to her husband, King Prasutagus, and although she had never driven it before she took it for a day out at the seaside. Chased by the Roman constabulary for 'twocking', and for driving without insurance she ran the roadblocks until she crashed into a tree, while using her rear-view mirror to fix her woad.

Unrepentant and unwilling to pay the fines, the Romans locked her up until she died in prison while eating a Pizza Romana, topping it and herself off with artichokes.

Her death lead to the OE saying, 'women and cars are a dangerous combo...' and ultimately leading to the law that allowed only men to drive horse-drawn and, in due course, horseless carriages.

It was not until 1897 that another woman, Minnie Palmer, was allowed to drive on British roads. And then it was only because it was her own car and French, unreliable, with only one forward gear. Another condition was that she was accompanied at all times by her hirsute husband wearing his beret and sitting on her right, in order to avoid her causing alarm to other road users.

More and more women realised that in order to overcome this restriction, they would have to disguise themselves in men's clothing, enormous goggles and fake or even real handlebar moustaches, a practice that lead to nationwide confusion in queues outside public toilets at motorway service areas.

Eventually, the authorities realised the only solution was to allow women to drive, with the proviso they were preceded by a man carrying a red warning flag. But this too was a short-lived arrangement, especially for the flag bearers, as it resulted in a shortage of conscripts for the First World War, especially when pacifist call-ups would suddenly and deliberately stop to be mown down by women drivers, in preference to the Hun.

And so, prior to World War II, compulsory driving tests and driving licences had to be introduced to ensure that enough men were available for the rematch…

———————

TfL Traffic Engineers have come up with a brilliantly simple plan to keep London's traffic moving.
Remove all parking spaces.

———————

BBC BROKEN NEWS: PASSENGER-LESS CARS

Police have urged the public to avoid travelling in driverless taxis after unemployed cabbies hacked into control systems and held passengers to ransom.

———————

My wife spends most mornings in the bathroom and if she misses a parcel delivery, she thinks nothing of chasing the postman down the road in her bath robe.

She caught him once, but he's fitter now, and faster.

HOMEBOUND
2009
Dan Dare

three plaster ducks

NEIGHBOURHOOD WATCH

Due to alleged government cutbacks the Metropolitan Police have announced they will no longer automatically respond to domestic burglaries.

I have responded by running down my Union Jack and removing my burglar alarm system and replacing them with a minaret and ISIS flag.

My house is now monitored 24 hours a day by local police, UK Counter Terrorism Unit, MI5 and SAS, and I save £30 a month.

———

Before I set off for work this morning, I used my wife's mascara to draw a Poirot moustache under my nose, and you should have seen all the giggles and raised artificial eyebrows I got.

———

The world is under attack by an invasion of mutant replicants. US.

———

FUTURE HISTORY

In a desperate attempt to alleviate congestion, London Traffic Engineers extend Congestion Charge Zone to the entire UK.

———

'Thou shalt have no other Gods before me',
said a rather insecure Almighty.

———

I think the best you can say about God is that he has been an under-achiever.

_____

Atheism is God's cure for religious hatred and conflict.

_____

THINK ABOUT IT...

If you are faced with twins, one a compulsive liar and the other compulsively truthful, how do you identify which is which?

You pick either one and ask the following question,

"If I were to ask your twin if you are a liar, what would his answer be?"

The reality would be the opposite to the given answer.

_____

You know your children are growing up when they stop asking you where they came from and refuse to tell you where they're going.

_____

In America, gun violence always seems to miss the most deserving targets.

_____

Most families have skeletons in their cupboards, but mine has several living ones too.

_____

He decided there was no future in being gay.

If the Earth had been flat, the oceans would have dribbled over the edges long ago, surely?

It seems that there are 'normal' people who actually believe that two penguins and two polar bears walked to the Middle East?

My wife thinks she's smart because it only took her a year to finish her jigsaw, when the box said 2-4 years.

I hope there is more to life than the hokey-cokey...

Humour is involuntary, and a humourist will still say the funny thing, no matter how inappropriate or offensive.

Instructor: "In fencing circles, Tracey, when we make a mark on our opponent, we say *touché,* not *gotcha...*"

When a politician says, 'I don't know', they are probably telling the truth, unless, of course, they do.

I believe that God created everything, except blind faith and stupidity.

The sexual revolution of the 1960's saw the invention of sex toys, such as the Ferrari 250 GT Cabriolet.

My publisher found my last book so funny he was laughing before he even opened it.

———————

If a black cat crosses your path, you can be sure it is going somewhere.

———————

Man's destiny lies not in the stars, but in the hands of every woman in his life.

———————

Poverty can only be temporarily reduced by giving poor people someone else's money until it's all gone.

———————

"Before I speak, I have an important announcement…"

———————

War allows governments to declare states of National Emergency and then curtail civil rights, even more so in civil wars.

———————

DIY ROADBLOCK

My wife has come up with a brilliant plan to divert speeding traffic from our street. She dons her hard hat and hi-vis vest, points her hairdryer down the road, and with clipboard in hand flags down every passing car, and carries out a vital traffic survey with a 'brief' ten-minute questionnaire...

———————

A proof tells us where to focus our doubts.

At his age my hedgehog Spike ought to know better, but he's got himself hooked up with a right little scrubber.

———————

I only joined Alcoholics Anonymous, so my wife wouldn't find out I still drink.

———————

When I heard you could still buy codpieces, I immediately grabbed the largest one I could find – the 6.2 litre AMG C63 Edition 507.

———————

"We choose to go to the Moon in this decade and do the other things..."

———————

How on Earth did man manage to land on the Moon on 20th July 1969 before the invention of SFX or CGI?

———————

A man's desire is commonly for a woman, but a woman's desire is more commonly for the man's desire.

———————

Never share a secret with a woman who is prepared to tell you her real age.

———————

Pompous student: I keep a notepad next to my bed so that I can jot down my ideas as they come to me. Is that something you do too, Professor?

Einstein: Not really, I only ever had one idea...

———————

SWEET DREAMS

Last night while dreaming, I woke up to find the wife had left me without even a note on her pillow. In fact, the pillow had gone too. Puzzled, I got up and checked her wardrobe, but no one there. I looked in the bathroom but that was empty as well. I looked everywhere – the kitchen, the laundry, the nursery, and the guest bedroom. I even checked the garage, unlikely though that was. Still mystified, I checked my emails, Inbox, Spam and Trash, and my voicemail and text messages. Nothing. So back to bed I went to finish my dreams.

When I awoke in the morning to that familiar smell of burnt toast, I realised the whole thing had been a dream.

———

Actually, my wife likes her toast 'well done', she says, the way her mother used to make it, whereas I like mine 'crisp and light brown'.

When it's served up burnt, I know trouble is brewing.

———

As Homer wisely once said, 'Words empty as the wind are best left unsaid.'

He also said, 'If you tried and failed, it was a waste of time and effort'.

(Sorry, that was probably Homer Simpson.)

———

"Where are you?" Godot.

———

WAITING
2007
Dan Dare

a solo performance

My wife is always on her phone, so I texted her to make an appointment for some conjugal activity, but her battery was dead and needed charging, she replied.

———

The next day I sent her another text on the same topic asking if she had any empty slots, but I think she still didn't get the message.

———

A week later, much to my surprise, I was awoken by a vaguely familiar hand struggling with the buttons on my pyjamas.

"What's going on," I asked, "feeling frisky?"
"Didn't you get my reply?" she whispered back huskily.
"No", I replied, to the accompanying knock on the bedroom door.
"Bugger" she said, "I must have sent it to one of the others..."

———

In response to the new world in which we live, new words are being invented every day, like *fintech* and *technostress*, or *tech-stress* for short, but at the same time many older words are falling into disuse, such as *very, man, woman, finishing school* and *truth.*

———

You cannot fool all the people all of the time, but half of them for four or five years is usually enough.

———

An election is no more than a Trojan horse race.

———

Purely by chance you understand, I happened across a list of the top 50 'openly' gay actors and was briefly surprised that apart from one, I had never heard of any of them nor did I recognise any of their faces, or their backs.

And then on reflection, I realised why not, and why they were on that list.

I went to see a clairvoyant, but she was closed, and then I wondered if she had seen me coming, or not.

An unemployed ventriloquist got a fairground job as a medium, and an old dear walked into his tent and said,

'I want to consult my dear departed hubby. Can you help me do that?'

'Yes,' he says, 'I can offer you three levels of service. For ten pounds, you can talk to me, I relay that to him, and then I relay his answers to you. For twenty pounds, you talk to him directly and he responds directly to you.'

'Well, that sounds perfect,' she says, and after a pause, 'but what is the third level of service?'

'Well,' he says, 'for thirty pounds you get the twenty pounds service while I drink a bottle of beer.'

I can recommend my wife's Scouse to anyone. It will bring you back to life or put you out of your misery.

UNCAGED

The energetic performance lasted 4' 33" from start to finish in almost total silence, with no applause even after the conductor had lowered his baton and fallen asleep...

———————

She: What do you want for your birthday?
He: Nothing really...
She: Come on, I have to give you something for your birthday...
He: Okay, how about a jolly good time, or if that's too much, maybe less of a hard time.

———————

After I realised that despite their spurious claims to achieve major environmental benefits, London's Congestion Charge Zone introduced by first Mayor, Ken Livingstone, had only reduced the number of vehicles by 5% but simultaneously managed to slow average traffic speed from 10.9mph to 8.8mph, and second Mayor, Boris Johnson's Cycle Superhighway network was the culprit for reducing that further to 7.4mph, resulting in London becoming Europe's most congested and polluted city, I decided my sentence was long enough to call it a day, and time to hang up my cycle clips.

———

Since the Tory faithful have given BJ the opportunity to do to the entire country what he did to London, I'm heading as far away as possible.

Antarctica looks rather attractive.

———————

STUPIDER?

When will feminists wake up to the fact that men are not very bright, a trait demonstrated by how easily they are fooled by dyed blonde hair, face paint, ridiculous shoes, silly scanties and eye-catching chests?

———————

Women often judge a man's character by the car he drives, and his financial status by that of his chauffeur.

———————

Women don't need to develop their DIY skills when there's a queue of men willing to lend a hand or two...

———————

DIY ESSENTIALS FOR LADIES

A man with a comprehensive toolbox and technical expertise.

And an accurate rule for checking his CV.

———————

My girlfriend asked me what it was that first attracted me to her. So, I told her,
"I think it was probably the irresistible classic beauty, razor-sharp intellect, sensitivity, wit, charm and my quiet modesty."

———————

As a young upstart, I thought my political convictions deserved more than a suspended sentence...

———————

I went to the doctor about my weight problem, and all she offered me were laxatives.

———

The following week I went back to complain about my excessive diarrhoea.

Dr A: Well, just how bad is it?
Me: It's so bad I daren't take my cycle clips off.

———

MASTER OF FAKE NEWS

Donald Trump claims yet again that he coined the phrase 'Fake News'.

———

NOSTALGIA 9

Remember the days when one could cross Europe by train with *haute-cuisine* in luxurious comfort on the Venice-Simplon-Orient Express.

Nowadays the most we can expect is the top deck of the Trans-London no.168 bus to Old Kent Road (Tesco), filled with the aromas and overspills of a McDonalds' skip after a busy weekend.

———

My doubts about the cheap carpet with free fitting were confirmed when the lump in it started to bark.

———

There's no use crying over chopped onions.

———

Beer Belly 1: Where's the missus tonight?
Beer Belly 2: I left her smokin' in bed.
Beer Belly 1: Yeah, that's the way to leave 'em.

————————

My pals think I'm under the wife's thumb, but I can tell you not only do I wear the trousers in our house, I wash and iron them too.

————————

NOSTALGIA 10

Remember the days when the primary use of Duck Tape was to keep the children quiet?

————————

SUBWAY BUSKER

"Thank you, folks, for listening to my saxophone and for your generosity that is funding the repairs to my spaceship that crash landed on your planet yesterday. You have enabled me to complete my mission and make a speedy return to my home planet, taking your President with me…"

————————

My missus was banging on about how much better women are than men at multi-tasking, but when I asked her if she would just shut up and sit down, guess what?

————————

My school was so tough we had our own coroner.

————————

What the hell are we doing in this Universe and why?

ASSET MANAGEMENT
2016,
Dan Dare

found photograph

My wife bought some of those 'speaking' bathroom scales but stopped using them after they winced and asked her to get off.

———————

His ability to please any woman whatever her nationality made him the world's most cunning linguist.

———————

Fifty years ago, I was probably one of the very first men to receive a proposal of marriage.
She said she would "but only if I married her", and well, you can guess the rest...

———————

BORED?

Try sneaking into a wedding and from the back of the church call out, "But I still love you."
Look over your shoulder, in feigned innocence, and wait for the drama to unfold.

———————

The missus threatened to leave me if I don't stop playing cards with the boys, but I'm going to call her bluff...

———————

What is posterity ever likely to do for me?

———————

I think therefore I must be René Descartes.

———————

Particle physics is quite complicated.

———————

A GOLD RUSH: 50 years of life, wife, and strife.

_____

I only recently discovered the real foundations of an enduring and robust marriage – corsets.

_____

Many a true word may be spoken in jest, but more true feelings are revealed in anger.

_____

The wife was diagnosed with a split personality, so they locked me up for bigamy.

_____

The penalty for bigamy is two mothers-in-law.

_____

My boyfriend accused me of being homophobic, just because I said I'd be buggered if I was going on holiday with him.

_____

I tried snorting Coke once, but the crushed ice made my eyes water.

_____

His enthusiasm for female company was so hard for him to contain it would often erupt to their squeals of delight.

_____

When I heard they'd found a cure for dyslexia I couldn't believe my arse.

_____

As a child I thought the Earth was flat, but as a young man I discovered otherwise, as opportunities appeared and disappeared over the horizon, and my life began to career downhill.

———————

My friend's teenage daughter informed her that ladies should choose a lipstick colour that matches that of their nipples.

I never knew that nipple-sticks even existed, although come to think of it, I have had the pleasure of some exotic flavours…

———————

Deleted by the Thought Police.

———————

I asked my doctor if she could prescribe something for my hypochondria.

She gave me a cocktail of injections, pain killers and laxatives, and said if I ever feel better enough to come back for more, she'd give me a bloody good hiding.

———————

He might have thought I had converted to Catholicism, but I was just checking I had my phone, wallet, spectacles and testicles.

———————

THE DIY ALPHABET OF BANNED WORDS:

A
Boy, Bank-robber
C
D
E
F
Golliwog
H
I
J
K
Letterbox
Man
Nigger, Nigga, Nigglet
O
Paki
Queer
R
Sambo, Sodomy, Stupid
T
U
V
Woman
X
Yid
Z

———————

"Sticks and stones may break my bones,
but names will never hurt me."

———————

I was in town last week waiting patiently while an LGBT demonstration marched down the street, and I wondered if the public would be as equally supportive if I were to 'come out' and declare my heterosexuality...

———————

I don't have any objection to people smoking in my company, as long as they don't exhale.

———————

Democracy is the tyranny of the majority, who hold an unsupported belief that they know what they want and are right more than half of the time.

———————

Boris was an amusing chap until he got into no.10.

———————

Some years ago I was at the London Art Fair loitering outside the Ladies toilets when Rory Bremner strolled past clutching a work of art he had just bought.

I said to him, "An impressionist, I assume?"

———————

He easily paid off his student debt with his credit card.

———————

I was damned if I could get a phone connection waiting for the concert to start. And I thought, if there is one place in the world where we all need some sort of signal, it ought to be in a church.

———————

I can't see the point in theoretical particle physics.

I have no problem with male-female role-reversal but I draw the line at childbirth and tampons.

———————

It used to be Cowboys and Indians, then War movies, followed by Cops and Robbers.

The next genre will almost certainly be 'Autonomous Cars versus Phonbies'.

———————

I expect humanity will finally expire when teenagers realise that real sex is no substitute for the 24/7, multi-orgasmatronic, 3D UHD CG VR augmented experience.

———————

A certain UK MP routinely lambasts other politicians and anyone who holds different views to his own as 'racists, neo-Nazis or fascists'. A case of crackpot or kettle?

———————

The one place in the world where one is guaranteed to find happiness is the lunatic asylum.

———————

Airport Gate Marshal: "I'm sorry, Madam, but you will have to put that exquisite but large chest in the hold…"

———————

I'm a bit worried about my wife since I caught her texting in her sleep. They were all *xxxxxxxx*'s

———————

A good book offers a route to immortality.

———————

20L DARK ENERGY
2014
Dan Dare

found empty jerry can

For my birthday I cracked open a 1998 vintage fizz that had matured in colour a little as expected but was dryer than expected. I thought probably past its best but rather than waste it, better to get wasted. So I did.

———————

Reluctantly, I have concluded that women are fundamentally dishonest, excluding of course those who never wear makeup.

———————

Why do the TV news channels insist on reporting trial verdicts as 'miscarriages of justice', leaving grieving families without their pound of flesh?

———————

I never knew the world was full of so many awful people until I joined Facebook.

———————

I was waiting for my train and heard three cancellation announcements in succession due to a person being hit by a train.
I wasn't sure whether it was one person hit by all three, or three separate people by three different trains.

———————

At my age, raising a leg to get into bed is a difficult first hurdle, but the thought of getting it over might be very tempting but is simply a move too far.

———————

A RECIPE FOR DISASTER

Two eggs, eight ounces of flour and a stick of dynamite.

I was on the bus the other day and had no idea that such people existed, except in pubs, TV game shows, adverts and horror films...

———————

ONLY IN NEW YORK...

On my way home after a night at the opera, I saw this large woman in black carrying a broom and I thought to myself I wouldn't want to meet you on a dark night.

I think she must have read my mind, because she hit me over the head with it and flew off in a rage.

———

Even at my age I'm not too old to be propositioned by a granny.
Unfortunately, I think she felt obliged to, after our brief but very close encounter in the overcrowded lift.

Her middle-aged grandson offered to give her away.

———————

It's an unexplained mystery why 90% of Canadians choose to live within 100 miles of their border with USA.

———————

I keep my headphones on in church every Sunday hoping God will speak to me. If he ever does, I'll be sure to give him a piece of my mind.

———————

When absolutely no one agrees with you, you can be sure you are absolutely wrong...or absolutely right.

———————

THE LAW OF UNINTENDED CONSEQUENCES

Action: Government imposes a charge for plastic bags.

Reaction: Shops abandon paper bags in favour of chargeable plastic ones, resulting in more plastic bags.

———

Action: Airport security prohibit the carrying of knives into aircraft cabins.

Reaction: People steal metal cutlery from airport lounges and restaurants or resign themselves to plastic cutlery and junk food standard of catering everywhere.

———

Action: Government bans people from travelling to Syria.

Reaction: Local economy declines further, problems deepen and spread to adjoining states.

———

Action: Traffic Engineers introduce one-way streets and turn-restrictions to improve traffic flow and capacity, and 'to improve safety'.

Reaction: Journey distances and times are extended and exacerbate congestion and pollution.

———

'The consequences of every act are inextricably included in the act itself.'

———

Sometimes I think the whole world is on a road to nowhere, which unarguably is ultimately true.

———————

In response to her scream from the bathroom this morning, I leapt out of bed to lay the bathmat on the floor so that she could get out of the shower.
I got a 'thank you' but no knighthood.

———————

> *'In days of old,*
> *When knights were bold,*
> *And toilets weren't invented,*
> *They left their load*
> *By the side of the road*
> *And rode away contented.'*

———————

My wife and I have been arguing about my funeral arrangements. I want a burial and headstone; she wants a cremation.

After last night's wilting performance, she's now decided she wants me stuffed, sooner rather than later.

———

It appears that somewhat earlier than expected, I have joined our aging sub-species, *homo semi-erectus*.

———————

After the success of Volodymir Zelensky in the Ukrainian elections, I think Peter Capaldi in his role as Malcolm Tucker should stand for Prime Minister…

———————

Romantically, it has been said that humanity is the product of previous generations of stardust, or in other words and less romantically, nuclear waste.

———————

Two decades ago it was thought that poor access to information was responsible for mass ignorance. The Internet has proven otherwise.

———————

I am often disappointed when my friends reject me and my opinions, but I just shake it off and find a new victim.

———————

I was tired yesterday and tired again today. I think it's time to retire.

———————

I left my smartphone at home yesterday and discovered the poet in me:

> *I wandered lonely without the cloud,*
> *Beside the lake, and beneath the trees,*
> *When all at once I saw a crowd,*
> *Waving and dancing in the breeze,*
> *A host of golden daffodils,*
> *But no damned phone to snap some stills.*

———————

I used to be an EU remain supporter, but after careful consideration I have concluded the only positive reason for remaining is that we would still have a veto.

———————

Sanity is only a question of statistics.

I was confronted by a beggar today. When I apologised that I didn't have any loose change, he told me that was fine as he accepted all credit cards…except Amex.

———————

Stanford's, the world's best map store, has recently moved from its prominent central London location to a nearby pedestrian alleyway. But I doubt you will find it without a map.

———————

You can choose your friends but not your family.

———————

During my first experience in a time-machine, it broke down and left me stranded in the Jurassic period, and by the time I managed to repair it and get it going again, it was pitch black and the fairground had closed.

———————

If little boys are made of frogs and snails and puppy dog's tails, whilst little girls of sugar and spice and all things nice, I think my missus has undergone some sort of metamorphosis.

———————

Following UK's classification of *'upskirting'* as a serious sex crime punishable by up to two years imprisonment and inclusion on the sex offenders register, Swiss finishing schools have advised their young wards that it is now safe again to wear black patent leather shoes.

———————

Iceland is a beautiful country, a bit like Scotland in places but without the Scots.

TIME-TRAVELLERS
2019
Dan Dare

unique photograph

I had planned to write a book that would change the course of civilisation until I realised that I am just as stupid as everyone else.

———————

The effect if not the purpose of political correctness is to narrow down the range of free thinking and free speech.

———————

'Wherever there is foul business there is always a woman involved.'

———————

Statistics are an easy way of converting sensible people to stupidity.

———————

Given Donald Trump's predilection for communicating on Twitter, perhaps it should be rebranded Twatter.

———————

It was undiplomatic of the UK's Ambassador not to run his reports to his employers past the White House first.

———————

Trump's unprecedented 'sacking' of the UK's Ambassador leaves the post vacant, which should remain so until there's an adult in the White House.

———————

God doesn't like Donald Trump but He's keeping shtum.

———————

My favourite chat-up line: *'Are you buying or selling?'*

———————

Many women dream of finding the perfect man, you know, the one who cleans the entire house while she enjoys her afterglow.

———————

NASA's big mistake with Apollo 13 was recruiting Tom Hanks who couldn't fly a balloon let alone a spacecraft.

———————

YOU COULDN'T MAKE THIS UP

On 21st May 2019, a man was found guilty at Cardiff Crown Court of possessing a Taser, a baton, cocaine, ecstasy and cannabis, and was warned that he was facing a prison sentence. His barrister asked if sentencing could be adjourned so he could go on his pre-booked holiday to Tenerife.
The Judge agreed as an *act of mercy'*, providing he came back...

———————

LOVE ISLAND?

I went to the doctor and asked her to examine my ears.

"What can you see?", I asked.
"Nothing", she replied, "but I can hear the sea."
"Nonsense", I replied, " that could be traffic or anything,"
"No", she said, "I recognise those South Pacific palm trees rustling in the breeze and the warm waves gently caressing my naked suntanned feet."

———

'Far away is close at hand in images of elsewhere.'

———————

Ticket clerk: Thank you sir, your privilege card gives you four free admission tickets...
VIP: Thank you, but I only need two - one for me and one for my bodyguard.
Ticket clerk, alarmed: Oh, my goodness, is he armed?
VIP: No, but her right hook is registered with the police...
Ticket clerk: Oh, I see, the wife.

———————

My Norwegian friend Truls' English is so good, he teaches it as a second language to illiterate Brits.

———————

TOO LATE

I was idling away a hot mid-summer's day after a liquid lunch and dozed off on the park bench, when out of the blue, I was awoken by an oddly dressed man.

"What planet is this?" he said.
"Earth", I said, "why?"
"What time is it?"
"About ten past five..."
"I mean the year?"
"Twenty nineteen..."
"Damn, that's fifty years past the end of civilisation", he said, as he disappeared, and I dozed off again.

———————

A fellow Master of the Universe and Time Traveller went back in time and successfully bumped off Fred Christ Trump, Donald's father. Unfortunately, it turned out to be a complete waste of time, for as we now know, from birth he was a real bastard.

———————

TAKING PRECAUTIONS

My first time-mission was back to VE Day in 1945 to sabotage the local condom factory, just in case…

———————

Alexa: "Good Evening, Dave, I'm afraid you just missed her last visitor, but I know where he lives..."

———————

Old dear 1: Hmmm, I need to sit down for a minute.

Old dear 2: Me too, I really need to get my weight off my feet.

Old dear 1: It's not my feet, I need to rest my chest on my knees.

———————

My constipation required numerous visits to the lavatory, but at least the problem was solved in instoolments.

———————

A friend asked me if I wanted to join her at the theatre to see Glenda Jackson in King Lear.
I said that I would rather rip my eyes out...

———————

My wife thinks too much is never enough.

———————

In my twilight years when I met the woman of my dreams and held hands with her, I suspect we were both just clutching at straws...

———————

At the age of 70, I had to apply for a new three-year driving licence. I had no health or eyesight problems, or previous driving experience, but on the last webpage of the application, I had to join, or at least consider joining, the government's voluntary organ donation scheme.

And, wondering whether a refusal would deny me a new licence, or if my organs were really mine, or only rented from the government to whom I would be handing them back when the time came, if not sooner, would I still qualify to drive without them. So I didn't join...

––––––––––––

THE 100 GRAND FINALE

I recently discovered that the current average cost of a simple funeral is around £5,000. If I live to reach 100 years of age, that cost is likely to have risen fourfold to £20,000. And in the likelihood of essential deployment of marshals or even the police to manage the expected 5000-plus crowd, adding a further £80,000, if not more, the total cost could well exceed £100,000, especially if live music, champagne and hostesses are to be offered.

So, until the end of the year, my publishers will be offering 1000 reserved premium seats that will include a raffle ticket for the opportunity to win my whoopee cushion, priority fast-track entry and one farewell drink each, at the heavily discounted bargain price of only £100 per ticket.

––––

At the end of the eulogy, I hope at least one of you will say, "Hang on a minute, I think he moved."

––––––––––––

DEATH STAR

Sunrise, Sunday, Ides of March, 1,001,001,001AD

THE END

JACK IDLE
2969
Dan Dare

aluminium plaque

ACKNOWLEDGEMENTS

I thank the following for their contributions, inspiration and the whoopee cushion...

Steven Appleby
Robert Armstrong
Keith Cass
Matt D'Arcy
Dan Dare
Albert Einstein
Aleksei German
Mel Hare
Tony Harrison
Ron Haslam
Bill Heine
Dyne Hudson
Mike Judge
Jonathan Monk
John and Emily Mortimer
Vera Mrdak
George Orwell
Gene Roddenberry
Donald Rumsfeld
William Shakespeare
George Shaw
Margot Lee Shetterly
Winston Smith
Robert Shrimsley
Boris and Arkady Strugatsky
Neil Turok
Geoffrey Willans
Christian Wolmar
William Wordsworth

EPILOGUE

May the following rest in peace, oblivious in their arrogance, ignorance, incompetence, stubbornness and stupidity:

Barnier, M.
Johnson, B.
Juncker, J-C.
May, T.
Trump, D.
Traffic Engineers

GOLD MEDAL
2004
Jack Idle

ABOUT THE AUTHOR

As a child prodigy repairing his mother's washing machine, Jack Idle succeeded in boosting its spin cycle to relativistic speeds, and so opened the door on the future possibilities of particle accelerators such as CERN's Large Hadron Collider, and of time travel.

Although now legendary, little else is known for certain about him, other than his name and birthplace, both of which are to be celebrated in 2946 with a laundrette that cleans stuff by reversing time.

In 2004 one of his several alter-egos was spotted at a UCL graduation ceremony collecting his *Master of the Universe* gold medal for his unilaterally acclaimed achievements in the fields of astronomy, astrophysics and cosmology.

Last year he came back to Earth, with his best-selling and visionary *Idle Thoughts & Other Stuff*, but forgot to remind humanity of the planet's impending doom a little over a billion years from now, an oversight now rectified in this latest book, actually written some years earlier.

Presently living in multiple times in the past and the future, which he hopes will allow him time to reconstruct Earth as a giant time-machine before time runs out, occasionally he returns to some of his old haunts, leaving a trail of dirty laundry and dismantled washing machines. If you have ever encountered such things on your own travels, you will almost certainly have missed their scientific significance.

Since he permanently lost his crayons in a runaway 'reverse spin cycle' experiment, this book doubles as a colouring book for those who cannot read or just can't be arsed…

HOW TO MAKE YOUR VERY OWN GOLD MEDAL

You will need:

- 1 metre length of 2cm wide gold ribbon
- 1 can of gold spray paint
- 1 x 7cm length of stiff garden wire
- 1 tub of plaster filler
- 1 or 2 self-adhesive paper logos of your own design
- 1 plastic coffee jar lid or similar, sized to suit your ego

You may need to enlist the help of a handyman (drilling of holes) a seamstress (ribbon sewing) and one or two glamorous computer-literate assistants (for production of the logos).

Assembly:

- Drill 2 small holes in the edge of the lid about 4cm apart.
- Insert the ends of garden wire into holes and bend to secure in position.
- Fill reverse of lid with the plaster filler to hold the wire in place.
- Spray the lid all over with gold paint and allow to dry.
- Cut out your paper logos and stick firmly onto the 'medal' faces.
- Thread the ribbon through the wire loop and sew the ends together.

Your medal is now complete.

Hang around your neck ostentatiously and watch your friends turn green with envy!

AN ORIGINAL COPY
2004
Jack Idle